DEVIOUS SENTIMENTS

poems by

James Capozzi

Finishing Line Press
Georgetown, Kentucky

DEVIOUS SENTIMENTS

ACKNOWLEDGMENTS

These poems appeared in *Blackbox Manifold (UK), Burnside Review, Denver Quarterly, DIAGRAM, The Literary Review, Maggy, Mayday Magazine, New Letters, New Orleans Review, The Offending Adam, Posit Journal, Radioactive Moat, Word For/Word* and *Zone 3.*

"Universal Description of the Known World Without End" was printed as an artist book in collaboration with Sandra Collins and Michael Loderstedt. "What Is the Meaning of This" is for Matt Burns and Jill Tominosky. The ending of "Proem" references Clive James's "On Seamus Heaney."

Endless thanks to Mary Jo Bang, David Bartine, Gisela Brinker-Gabler, Joanna Penn Cooper, Shawn Jasinski, Bernadette Mayer, Adam Piette, William V. Spanos, Cody Todd, Joe Weil, Bob Wilson, and Monique Zamir for their support.

Thanks also to the Vermont Studio Center and Woodstock Byrdcliffe Guild for the peace and quiet.

Publisher: Leah Maines
Editor: Christen Kincaid
Cover Art: Kingsley Ifill — "Soul Swallower"
Author Photo: Howard Romero
Cover Design: Casey Capozzi

Printed in the USA on acid-free paper.
Order online: www.finishinglinepress.com

Author inquiries and mail orders:
Finishing Line Press
P. O. Box 1626
Georgetown, Kentucky 40324
U. S. A.

Table of Contents

Comedy is a man in trouble.
                    —*Jerry Lewis*

I.

Hard Times

after Prevért

last year's crop was vile and hard

a vice we indulge
for this country

come on rats and mole-rats
times that shred us so

we know our part

we're bolted, finished
as the radishes

our urn leers
we swear to baroque firmament

a parade of vermin's coming

a menagerie
of paupers

marching to our death
and glamour

voice of the rich in our ear

superrich: a banner smiles
above your battlement

two points chained
by a parabola

it's June man this is war
don't you see it

our rage yokes the fields like kudzu
yet this country persists

sirs yet I come to tell you of
my patrimony

my grandfather's passage
lashed to his brother

in the hold of some boat
that was sturdy like an ashtray

is our joy and death
it is our share

of course you measure your uberriches
with our children under a sword
and your moccasins nearby

your modes and opinions

fizzle like spit in a fireplace
throw sparks before a portrait
of Antonio Ulloa

your travels by river

jangles of your heirloom scabbard
are music
rattling our skulls and toes

rattling our teeth

and bracelets we schlep
to entice your women
out of their corsets

or moment of silence

their voices like a boot
feel good as they pass through us
so we allow them to trespass

what a piece of crap is man

superrich we meet again
the Legacy Homes
of your French Quarter

we commend you

for your coal chute and dumb waiter

holler holler *sirs!*

to no avail—the rich have eaten already

our crop is this country's misery
we gnaw on it like donkeys do

our face continues *fait accompli*

to say what you say
stay you indoors with your luxuriant genitals
and mink oil

your   machinations

one day we turn you into taxidermy
with a moussed pompadour
an era of mope and claustrophobia passes

a trombone announces the river's new

path south to the sea
via buoy

a harbor opens and implies a peace

if only
to appease us

for our part we like to pretend

that new vistas are nigh
that chiggers on our horse go up in flames
O what a boon it is

these are good times

in our cesspool village
our murdered language
between two dings in a manmade river

time impinges on our horses

time does not remember us
sucking dollar drafts

or some bread or a turnip

I resemble an ox

my uncle was the world's most unclean bum
my father was an exile in the mountains
boxed by permanent séance

this whole world's pervaded

by good gods slumming our paddocks
I owe my life to the C Suite
I owe my life to the God of the Sea

I owe my life to landlords and dead cops

soldiers jockeyed by duty
our séance is permanent
like this a spectacle begins

Lux Mundi

at the same time
a woman flops on a vinyl stool

and begins her disquisition
on the cigarette/tobacco tax

her logic grows mesmeric
then unlocks, a quasar above

the city, in all its criminal glory
desires of the emerald ash borer

run amok in a lumber yard
near the rat's nest bar

in which we drink and sit
gas lamps fuming

copper bracelets on her forearms
found in an abandoned factory in Buenos Aires

my Bic and lung
which I know by now is luminous

her voice precedes a madness
the whole world must participate

In the City of Sociopathic Draculas
you walk as one among them.
Sunlight down an avenue
fires your profile in a bankface:
not without a rehearsed calm
and brio, a way
you posit your jaw against an hour.
The city in this hour
between two stupors
yawns, careens forward
paws you
with its underwater buslight.

Night falls in the industrial zone.
You ride in
silence to meet your friends
but when you arrive at the marina
they're already wasted.
They try to eat, but the food
falls from their mouths.
Everyone's staggering around
repeating themselves
so you go back to your
decrepit duplex
with a view of the river.

All your self disfigured in this
house: sessile, brain only
eye roving on a stalk.

you wake up

Market rot begat this house
and, through this house, its resident.
Mornings, a ruined joist makes noise

under an antique desk
its wires and levers
looming like

beyond your mutant understanding—
vestigial, no symmetry
but thudding just the same inside

a map of hell

the detached jar your skin's become.
Where, sure only of the life of one's own
words, you cough 'em up, cry blood.

the movement of
the river lights
the wall

asleep in a room with no windows or walls
basted by the city's voice

from the agora's fugue a mason appears
to slash you with a spade

or crumple your skull with a stone
because of your language, politics, face

it's that other face, the cotton one, turns
toward shore-of-the-bathers
surrenders to sun

until hair, flesh, eyes burn & peel back

& your charred shadow
rises with claws where the hands were

to kill Time flying in the palms

stay for good in this
volley of bats, threat-admixed-with-pleasure
sum rhythm of sticks beating laundry
power washer roaring on a hovel

momma named you after a king

all for you, the assassin's fist
a mason's face like a shovel

River of the world don't do much either
to cheer one up.

Men drive calves from pens
to doors like smoking mouths.
Downriver a pumphouse breathes out

dirty orphans scheme
falls applaud.

En gran Teatro Colón
plumes of smoke go
from the gallery up into spotlight

black and white
affirming life.

Into this breath visible
the mesmerist inquires: good people
why do you kick like a calf with its neck split?

How do you cry with your throat opened?
Doesn't this world persist

in thinking your name
and the coy laundress
as she steps into the train

that leaves for the country
at sundown?

At night you
ramble down planks

laid end-to-end
on sucking mud

past the stockyard
into a "town"

razed and rebuilt
four times by fire.

At night policia
preach at a pyre

rising from the plaza
while one man in

a poncho
skims shark-like

the mob.
Society has this

anarchic streak
running just under

its surface like a shark.
You feel it, mob-borne

(the inflation of his ribcage)
because night is tactile

and erotic. Droning
cant and photo poses lift/

desist. An us emerges.
The imagination also

holds him up at his cache
of pamphleture

and camouflage
smoking dust

before an effigy
of Pedro de Mendoza.

You follow after
his swale of red hair.

In the morning the two of you
commit adultery in the sea.

I don't know when it started.

I was a child, that's all
I remember. The *power*

of our courtyard—

its plums, thyme. The shrub that wept
when we petted it.

My brother Sacha

blew in his enormous voice
for more delicious lychee.

We played dead among the statuary.

At night
the sky turned black

so we could sleep.

Finally in a film
my stone boat waits for me.

The sea is calm, sky

vacant. The sea is calm
and transparent. I have been

waiting to pull iodine air

into my lungs, to soak them.
I raise an oar—

look, a dolphin. A cloud with the horizon

in it, that's all I remember.
Like a kid I run to tell you

how stupefied I am.

What Is the Meaning of This

raga of crickets / scanner squawk
demonic noise at night
hacked-at poison sumac tangle
train eye glazed & smothered in graffiti
town grown iffy / lately unstable / into the realm of verisimil
tub of Crisco life force feeds you
gopher the citizen kicks to oblivion / beats with a tomato stake until it truly suffers
"hey you don't like it move to the fucking country"
stranger's scrawl all over you / whatever they write in Erie & Albany /
            Scranton Elmira
escape from these places covered in these places / toting a book about the citizens
living close / together but separate like modern democracy
smear of gore willed by absentee landlords
night in which they grab dumb forms & make them speak *right now*
subject of the text's predictive tendency / not yet out the dark
mannequin in a shopping cart / single stoplight blinking
cop that climbs surrounding hills to check for lightning strikes / reason for this site
to ignite
            itself four times
source for ignition / decision to risk our life
Golden Rule Lumber House drowned & torn down / & elsewhere in town
            its arsonist circling you
not apart but parallel

Probably, Socrates

Shouldn't it happen at dawn
    when a squatter retires to the gravel lot
where his staked tent's powered by orange extension
cords chained through the dog door
                      of a darkened house?

If one garbage crew convenes in the dark
    does it not find two men burned badly in the park
and wild ferns on a freeway median
sagged toward damp earth?
                Let first sun shear down.

Its iron findings defile the magnetic feel
    of night. Let one report
to morning shift at the ruinous motel, strip sheets, scrub suicides
bludgeoned by memories.
        For is not memory, as source of all remorse, a cudgel?

And pale sky above fairground amusements
    if one, seeing right through it, finds oneself
divided by invisible force, as iron filings define a magnetic field?
Say the time has come.
            What is the question one must ask?

If we are ruthless in the daytime, veering at an obscure coda
    "What?" is the question one must ask
in the spirit of progress
destroying the self of two hours ago
    who was an idiot and a coward.

Binghamton

Binghamton
like the fin of a tremendous eel
the voice of your citizens
rustles in its cave

and your citizens wait you out
one foot broken, in our trucks
we wait outside the bar and tug our dicks
   when the shot girls break free

and your citizens get tasered
your citizens don't complain
   we bring it on ourselves
for flesh, in suspension   is glorious

we feel the oily river moving over us

river from hell, crippled fountain
blotch of the sun
dollars austere and disbursed

phosphoresce, and lure us who have
slid into this dark arena
   out

crack smokers, sucker punchers
crawlers up from Jurassic slime, I ask you
   when
is the fix not in

O neighbor
what time does the epiphany begin

Le Brut

Casey, move it
Casey
We've got to move it
We are two travelers
Two travelers
So move it along
Step into the multitude
Like this   it parts
   Claro
You are meant to disembark
In stained glass windows of the sea
Casey, move along
In gashes
In the wounds of this world

Or else forfeit your living in the world
Casey
We're going
Be strong
We're losing
& you have been sloppy & weak
No sleep for years, beginning now
If you quit you quit on the world
A little trip's the least you can do
A tour in
The tears   where we get going
   Casey
We are the polis & this
Will not pass

Casey the people are cooked
& nobody will change it
Our yolk is broken
Body prehistoric
Our talons are lopped short
Yes life's question is beautiful and it hurts
The quest for justice is defunct

Casey
Our place
Is still our place
The quest for justice is shot
But soon we will arrive
& mend all
Who need mending

Soon we will arrive
They need an ending
Save them already
I'm ready
To push the issue
What is the question
Casey people are mainly
Water & somebody must cleanse it
Like a wand we'll find the river
Clatter & make headway in the fields
It's our fate   to remake
Our one body
That is what I think of us
That is all I want for me

Not to Touch the Earth

I know, James, the premise of the earth—Jesus's body, crop of corn.
All his pain and misery, all his viscera, blooms inside of cobs.
All that animates our fields began in miniature.

I don't know if it's fated or saved or free, the coming crop
only that it's blue, color of our veins, color of our human lips

    with which we chant and kiss.

Our mouth shall be full of corn and rice
and every evil effaced—pure winds exorcise our corn, no despair
or boredom taints it.

    No danger. The corn's soul is the sun.
The moon's soul is the ocean, swollen like a field in August

    or silo full of horse-corn

levitating between two moons.
Faithless James, unquiet James
    your anger, the gleaners, the phases of the moon

pass into fields of corn
    and the corn leans, cries out.

Its maze collapses in piles of silk and husks.

The Dream of Endless War

is the dream of Solís
Espartaco
José Tomás

El Juli
Luis Vilches
El Cid

the dream of endless war is the one
with El Cid
El Juli

& Ortega Cano's
warring
even in mountainous regions

even in regions you can't begin to conceive
a medieval dream commands
Diego Ventura

& Eugenio Mora
not mauling them outright
but yanking them from their graves

with faces
no voice
or vice versa

what have they done to deserve this
dream of Solís as infinite shiv
the people as revolting mob

cannot desist, casting themselves
extras by the thousands
against barricades at the coast

no conscience left

at the country's center
is its capitol & motto, slathered in

Joselito
Luis Domecq
César Matías Girón

every one growing harried & desperate
you gotta watch out
they don't rest

you have to look out everywhere
in Cádiz
Ronda

beneath the station at Jeréz
anything becomes tradition, any time
the senator's tintype

& filibuster
his daughters green with joy, no agita
vascular herds dragging out valleys

pull citizens in pairs through the graves
at Arcos, Olvera
white Conil

Carmona's ruin
in an inhuman
heat

also Estepona fleet's
anarcho-backpacker collective *ab ovo*
camp & harangue with no pot to piss in

as in Santander or
Setenil's psychic

caves

painted, floating
to Zafra or Rocio
Victor Puerto, Vilches, Espartaco

can never be at home on this earth
they bleed through walls to outlands beyond the city
where we arrive & separately think to ourselves

I've been acting strangely
where we roam by river live fauns foam
& stammer in cages like a natural drum at dusk

the sun staged low in a lantern's light
an orphan legend of the region
know the earth turns away from it

know the country won't let Solís be
himself, at peace
not proxy for us

hybrid at some border
of course it's a river but broken
running backwards

through a future like a faun's
prodded, ridden hard
by zealots

I give you all the evidence
every fodder falls together
to a meadow beyond city walls

where we walk up red lanes
wide & blazing fungus
blades scraping out a carcass

red guts trotted out
beyond all knowledge of ourselves
& the fields exhumed too much as expected

it's already catching up
with us the time is early
evening end of August

shafts of light lean down against
us & we are no longer as walking
temporary with each other

Still, Loneliness Kills Them

better to wait
for a rider skates
in and out of star
light, shadow of
saguaro, drawn on
ward through zones
devoid of music, merely
cactii screaming
under an axe—I
by my intestine
am tethered to
a dune that's got
promise
and that's what matters
approaches a lone rider
the desert's air
brushed on
the side of her van

now I'm an animal
eats its tail

already in summer
shagged and muggy
I emend my body's specter

already in the windbreak
I snack

but what kind of creature is this
what has been created
here in these fields

infested with geese and cicadas
sound of the county's

business in my ear

sure trucks roll in
and out but I don't

see much
hay I smell, clover

spark no pang
dumb as an erection
now am I

an ouroboric *type*
chump for this vernacular

(I'm running out
of ways to ask
the question)

desire is an invisible industry
    it chokes the entire valley

stars emit an ethereal fluid
    in this whorl

from top to bottom
    no one knows you

mist anoints the fish house
    no one knows you

you who have
    your purpose

you who
    must leave us behind

II.

Universal Description of the Known World Without End

For Bill Spanos

to begin with this—
        the mind in the world
              is a labor
        like the angry fabula you stage

no ultimate view from the eternal
                stratosphere, choked by ether
though we do harry incessantly
           the body

        it cannot be made
        to cohere

to begin with this   dispersion
           of our high seriousness
  & spinning outward from that we know best
        the world is the case
the imagination saps
           its apprehension via
      language/the occasion
    live & finite
          cast always headlong down
          like
             white sun light

to begin with these   ephemera
       for rearranging wandering into
though we don't know what we look for
       & will never know

to love life by thinking
         it's absurd, I think
     without context or politics
my body a cluster of clusters
          of metastatic cells

only in opposition is anything created
    in a quarrel between equally
                viable positions

not to the death   where one defeats the other

      they belong together, unreconciled
          but open, deepened

in thought at one with feeling   at home
      in time limits

            & space limits
      the crude contingencies of life

there's an order in the world
                that does not close down/
        preclude possibility

does not project a drama in excess
trigger an emotion so massive so deep

                it annihilates the body it contains

example
the blowhole at Telde is terrible, sublime
      you go to Telde to tame it
                    you live in the mist

    & paint it, perpetually

time is just an appearance
                 truth is utter permanence
what created this world is confirmed in the next

      is overwhelming, threatening life itself

you pay a price for beauty
      & form   you're pathological, pursuant of
                    a place in the whole

a man atop his blowhole is a god
everything in its place where he put it

                  he put himself there, above the surface
that's foamy & blasted to shreds
               an immense panorama

      an anarchy without end

was not, for the Greeks, chaos
but a conduit—

      gods running all through these Greeks

time (dissemination of)
when you stop it it's no longer time

lobbed not placed into
the world

everything's strange & uncanny
        crucial to your laughter, thus

nothing causes your anxiety
           or nothingness

something must cause your fear
           some thing

you have ways of managing
                you can run from it or kill it

the Puritans began this process
          by periodically wiping out the Pequots

King Philip's Wars
        a work ethic emerged

getting impossible to live like this   in crisis

you have every right
& responsibility to remake history
                    it cannot account for squat

here among the huts and scuzz   the text generates
                    a question—

          who is this You?

you is an alcoholic, seven feet tall
wearing a straw hat & leather shoes

you voted for John Kerry seven times
& are perhaps overly fond of vegetables

that might have something to do with something

or you don't eat, you don't sleep
it impoverishes the soul you say, half-joking
        the county lays you like a monk into its stream

you name every stone   made simple   the bed inhales
        water crushes in the gaps

Essex County fathoms you deep within its secret mind

            doubt empowers your prayer

it keeps you everywhere
           behaving certain ways

you is Virgil

                hoarse from long silence
reciting your myth in relation to the old ones, the ideal cities

       you need to go through dead worlds to escape

deranged by time, demonic time
            the corrosive methods of a clock's time

symbolically, the sea's
            forestructure   guides you

                through close dune grasses

undermines you always with blades & etchings
            of the grass itself

you barely manifest, are barely resolved
                or even given definite shape

        a morass between two states

taught either/or
    not both/&   & so on

what is the poet's insufferable condition
confronted with a world of fugitive images

        anxiety without object

how can one accommodate the lovely grave to Capitalism
eject from this parceled world

into a nirvana
between time gone by

& to come

there are two routes

                                one is good

one generates   *escapism*

our paycheck, our aphorisms
                  eventually become disturbed

what are we missing
                  what can't we take hold of

             does it not unite heaven & earth

shall our psyche be mourned   *our mind*

                how will our image live

dissatisfaction sets in

our families decay & take to the hills
                project themselves onto a land

                we build or dismantle to liberate
                an ancient diversion

     sitting at a desk to make a world

don't ask, let's go
           into this infinite progress, infinite regress
           our circular, erosive boredom

we never arrive
           our Sentra leads us in a variety of directions

we come back to our families   if at all
          ill, a little pious
                              but hungry that way

with speed we come already in a downpour
          spill our guts irregular in the distance

          not reckless but   funereal

way back in our consciousness, plumeria
                              startle us
                    out of deadness

                              & entropic deer
                                        still there, though spectral
                    haunt us/tend to dominate

Jesus
the daily life of every single living thing

you think about it as much as possible
you write it all down

you don't wait

you don't suspend your consciousness until
you arrive at what you're waiting for

the start is always now

a logic has spoken for us
        we might not know it

our memory undermines us
history supplies us
                with Spanish & Roman archetypes

  an army of nasty swans & savants
the fright that is our privilege in this world

  the threat of the polis, the henchpeople
even in their sleep more vicious than ever before

the invisibility of the hitherto visible
        suffering of the natives
                        so close to the surface

    we feel it as if it's the way things are

our effigies—unhomed, exploited, feared
have always known these things

they fish but do not farm
        roam but do not occupy
range do not inhabit

they beg us to make their lives better

the effigies cry out together
we must change our life

  at work all night eternally despite us
threatening always to embrace us

      our hand in their throat is at work

my wife was an exilic figure
   she   knew what those in the community don't

   was not put into the world by a plot
or into a plot by the world

between her life & the earth was
           an art, not the truth

an oak tree, stupid
no consciousness, no conscience

but the leaves seemed to smile
we'd head out toward the trees

to beg for mercy
for a grace that was *there* but invisible

some sort of war thing
         had infiltrated our memory

we lay helpless in the road

III.

Procession of Cervantes's Hand over the Bridge at Lepanto

1. Timbers fall in line.
2. The part with the infants.
3. The fountain's square, festooned with Spanish weapons.
4. Two Christians in huts, Brotherhood of the Sainted Secret,
       become sixty Christians in crisis, abandoned
            with conical hats.

5. Dressing and disparaging the Consecrated Stag.
6. Confrontation of the League of the Wound by a passel of
       consumptive earls.
7. The Christian Brotherhood, pulsing between columns, implores us.
8. The end of asking nice.

9. Procession of a reliquary jam-packed with faces,
            lips drawn back and desiccated.
10. Priests fume in causal doorways.
11. The Order of the Three Necessities extols a stooge.
12. The one in the middle is base, depraved.

13. Plumeria emit a narcotizing haze.
14. The sierra's stare, tan with chaparral, surveils our fearful
       beating on a ledge above a river.
15. Packs of beagles coalesce in the manner of tzarist speech,
       frenetic and surreal, red with weals and sores.
16. A lizard like a mouth recedes in its branch
       and umbra of the figure in a peasant hat, mustache, machismo.
            Over-sexed. His wife (our sister) is pregnant. The river (its rise)
       scares her—how it tumbles and recedes, is integrated like a mind.

17. Allegorical passage of the Knights' Triumph Over Fish.
18. The pilgrims get along, but a *dark* pervades our mannerism,
       the resentful way we share sardines.
19. A cross flocked with birds, hearts of angels.
20. A century of Spaniards and also police, preceded by a drumline.

21. My face no longer speaks, but sails through the houses
       of its rounds like a hex, witch of its religion.

22. Through holy doors holy forms repair themselves.
23. Corporation is our funeral
24. So I leave, under the eerie calling of the wolves.

Bride of Paradise

Here, too, the gods represent
　　　　　　　—Heraclitus

as a litany of fields
perfected in their season
margin burnt where a farm begins.

Enlisted to an ethics
in your Nikes and sweats
I watch you march into ragwort

as per my wishes:
my cash is tied up in trees.

As an alien nation arrives within
the larger one, with apples
       and patois born from raw dirt.

I get up every morning, step into my boots
ride my hand over the dog.
Fry an egg and shave while the radio talks.

I got a lot of stress. I work with an ominous rasp
in my chest, carving Big Black River into Oregon, orchards

      swollen with hives and cabins. Trees.
Articulate pickers, lashed to my branches, are thieves—
      their adam's apples bob all evening under seeping nectar.

From the darkened treeline they dream me, as a man's flannel moving
      with great style before a stand of pines, a man who is all self
capable of anything

though if I sleep the river chokes to death
      cash crops collapse to dust, bees die off en masse.

I live like this throughout the night.
I continue to inhabit my life.
I can't help but suffer its crisis every morning before sunrise—

hour of the predictive dream, they say.
In an omen of their materials and tools
      muttering a little, I wake to sounds of the workers scraping

on the docks, where they trap crabs
                    and crack them with their hands.

On the docks where they get jobs
                    expression of America.

On the docks they distribute ephemera
pamphleteering with a slogan and bonfire
                    to make the docks fulfill their promise.

It's a seminal time, their body mostly
beholden to an august force, dog and tarp
until night falls.
                    The cannery also decays.

They can't wait to fly away from the shame of the coast
under silver trees, and arrive

on an errand not unlike vengeance
                    for the country's born liars.

The forest's lies cohere
            as *a suicide*, a thing
drowned in a foot-deep pond, buried
                by petals we sprinkle on after—
        abjected ourselves
by a poem of *elegy* and *prayer*, gathered in that
        fetish for performing our humanity.

Once in woods behind my mother's house
        a pack of dogs jogged toward me
doggedly
                I thought.
        Its causelessness revealed *a destiny.*
Scattered into watershed, outskirts of North Jersey
        students, the poet was alive. Scared but ready to die.

When twilight raked its hunchback I knew I'd never be free

as the centaur appears, with beak and casque
bashing down brush where it go.
As a premise in the forest, roving above

us in its shadow, eating always, the centaur live with lice
matted fur made powerful with parasitic life.

Pickups plow gutters, on-ramps toward Seattle
where the centaur always settles: undersea, as damage
to a port the city's too cash poor to fix. It hunts this world

so I kneel down before it with raingear
and duct tape protecting my body.

When the centaur rocks back and forth, its city comes apart
at the seams. Flayed by rain, cars ripping past, boxcars colossal
hammering down tracks

mountain near, cone blasted
O Seattle this is it!

One barely survives the rust belt, hell-hole metaphysics
of upstate New York and would rather dismiss its every omen
and event, except for

K as depression-era workhorse, bred by her master to save
all our lives, dusky mane swaying back
and forth like Fortune itself.

Or a crow pecking puddles of pink barf on the sidewalk,
their source certainly deceased, where
the crow stands for us, the vomit the city, the city its economy.

Or the crow for the State, the puddles us, the city Bill's riot act.
Either way, we're in there someplace
with possibly seconds to live.

Shauna, down from Albany on a Tuesday in her Audi,
though I walked home numb, no thoughts or skull or spine.
Asphalt peeled from the ground.

A genius pedaling past hissed *heads up, asshole*
disappearing into pointless snow.

Next day, Yule Log crackling, Shawn and I on his sofa
ruminating about the textual attitude.

Shawn: the attitude's disastrous, wallowing
in genre sleaze, acting up in bad faith,

overfed in every direction.
But our allegiance to the question, our endurance, is a heroism
I said to him, repeatedly.

The text's a compromise, I sez, with dignity.

Thee bears, dolphins, working animals never get plugged in
to this bleakest street
in America. The neighbors
behind their Xmas decoration
are dead. Lights winking in their circuit beg
avenge us
fists in pockets, keys laced through fingers
emptied onto Main Street.

There the bar churns out furnace heat, prewar rambler
gets a brand new coat, stone foundations hold. We live for this,
more or less. Someone might bust in on us high in the office, slumped under
a framed postcard of "Maximo, champion high diving dog of the world"
flung from his plank, into blank space with eyes rolled back.

I ask you this: how much solace can you stand?
Do you want to be some ghoul in search of the perfect meal and a dream home
                    extending your life all over a road between two worlds?
One here, where snow lays its hand across
our many mouths, and another in the skies, where I sail around
to parties in heaven, dancing too hard, smoldering peripherally, thinking
your name nonetheless and always
with devious sentiments.

Poem Called "On the Figure and Its Realities"

in which Tony calls the vegetables "refreshing"
though they aren't a swim or a drink
or wind off of my visions of Lake Washington   *they've always been responsible*
with sky painted over it
and pines refracted onto it   *sub-mental*
squadron of fragile biplanes.
Tony, you call them as they plow down   *or freight they send out*
refreshing, and I see what you mean
but your smug gourmetizing won't sit right   *around themselves*
too much smothers this occasion
and this occasion suffers, hamstrung, lamed.

My memory of the city is my body.   *in waves*
Every lung and synapse is Seattle's
sound of water, grafting knife, apartment with
ambient sobbing (vista skyline, sound   *the port emits*
Cascades). At night freighters raise their waterlights
past Alki—the working pier, with creosote
and freight, invokes a longing longer than all others.   *sometimes the country itself*
Salmon slither among pylons, live
down there forever, if only to remind me that
the city held me like an aunt.   *by frigates*
Was kind to me, though I was not kind in it.

For years I walked in the alley
of the halfway house, lot of the car-sized sinkhole   *here there be*
shadow of the condemned bodega, then
shoved the door in. The drinkers have already begun   *the labors of*
their monologue. Their lamps and monologue wash over
refresh us. We have already begun to make our way   *the laymen*
down a short corridor
the twilight exits refresh us   *kinetic and dispensable*
into a pantomime
and patio where our crew endures   *everything makes them understand*
in vice, watches for us, goes *yo look who it is.*

I Had No Periplus

Countrymen I come to tell you
not in the cadence of a Roman Senator
but the mumbles of one crouched
and flogging mud with a stick
that is to say naked
that is to say at risk
of sounding like
the fantasist I am

my great-grandfather's Ellis Island manifest
read *occupation: peasant*
and I mistook this so ecstatically
for a pedigree I quit my job
making the good people of Seattle
laugh all fucking night
and scourged this earth
elated, scared, insane
for a decade.

Now ten years on, deposited at Ulan Bataar
in the Tuul's glory I see
myself reflected, at work, inane
raking walnuts beside a yurt
that burns terribly
like a memory or monk that never fades
and is no consolation.

The Moon Is a Painted Stone

The Muse is a room you find under cork trees
near an abbey's door, reeking of horseshit
and oranges. Valerian. Study of the Muse requires
quietude, so you place the barrel in your ear

and blast your way inside, made implicit in its angles
its diptych depicting a saint pursued and named
by her sin. Not why or when, but *there*—the world's road.
A throng of leather puppets makes its evil

rounds on it, below the cliffs, among the rocks. Their heads are
a wet blur. Your own brain gone, you're
deaf with stone and painted air

so she sails into ocellated oaks and notes that
your obsequity is nothing like humility. That
the whole is greater than the part.

Dream of the Zombies

in which I
conspicuously Aryan
am harried by
the citizenry

pass my hours
as in life
lurking through hallways

unsure who'll rush me
famished next
from panoramic gore

the worker
of Anna

her mohawk & rugby leg
her bow mouth
her bottomless mouth

or Max
with his big sister
and activated gang

smashes in
my house's poor
construction

I slam a hatchet
into all their skulls
and stir

though these infected don't
seem overly worse off

they swear to me they're cursed
in another, later house
where we all suffer horribly from thirst

Western Bronze Display

  Like fiddle or the firmament you are free to the core,
     gleaming with salt.

  You are free to the core and deep lung.

  Evening tells me you are odious,

  but as tar clots down walls in December and January
  breath thinks and turns over into language

  by a bridge, each day, as smoke, keeping time.

Days recede on trawlers with algae.
Inside the gorge a Ditch Witch rusts.

Iguanas ascend fan palms when
sun rides down to whitewash them.

We ascend a parking deck in circles.
You soar in a jet, surrounded by sad babies.

Chaste action of macaws at their seeds:
everyone knows the macaws are in danger.

I saw one with a leg off and its eye torn out
but at night while I sleep, the bird the lizard

the soot fog sea convene in a clearing
and are remade by god.

Cross the marina in darkness, bucket of water poured

into water. Two men leave as a pair to drink beer like men
        on fire, hands torn

open and brown. Boards crack under the lithe one.

Schools tilt and rise in the swells, pelican splayed on a skiff
        swivels to ask

What is it you're writing?

"Cross in the morning to Animas, La Boca. The beach
        at Bucerías a machine for lifting water."

Why are you sweating? Have you been drinking?

I weigh 400 pounds.
And yes.

End of vista, bathers, boats. End of steam off of food:
no oysters no crabs.

End of food, bathers, venturing in the bay

where the vote and parity end. Birds on a branch
end up party to the tzar's descant. No dogs.

Dogs end their lost hunting when a wave wipes cathedral steps:
end of nose end of hope.

Sunslaves stop their flagellations, blotted by a wave beneath
the seat where Wayne sat in jeans,

on perpetual general strike.

No trees here. Hacked them all to firewood.
No trees, no contract, no work.

Eels colonize these ponds themselves.

It's natural to see a duckling taken under by an eel.
When ducks and swans overbreed, eels preserve a balance.

The eels refill drained ponds in weeks. Their mucous coating keeps them
undiseased as they squirm from the bay
through damp grasses, pond to pond in waves.

It's important they lay out in the waters
these early histories

and whether or not we mount them as ornaments
in canisters or wallets.

Fissile movement, a mutiny
eats grain each day, little by little. Even the eels eat acid.

You in a Spanish place. The year out of order.
Only a tent city stirs each morning, more nothing.

Houses of the valleys
mostly stone, flat-roofed, and low.

Walls thick to protect against wind and storms.

Men lay beams from wall to wall
on top of these a mat of canes

on top of these flat stones.

Mica hauled from mountain streams
must be laid under a Jupiter in retrograde

says Wayne, eyeing the storm's mess

moving over roofs
stomping clay into the gaps.

A vision of you taking
pictures in a dress, sobbing in frustration and sadness,

like a tic bisects us spread out half-in-sun, sound of the workers tapping.

Hollow pole dragged over asphalt. Gas truck come round, jingle blaring,
bangs across a bridge of planks and beachhead

spiked with storm debris. A woman selling pies goes

it's just one thing after another after another
then keels over.

Her husband's perched above the sea,

smoking on a crate with his pit lashed to it,
thirsty for our throats, tearing at its chain

even when way down the beach we reach the last bend and look back.

It barks roughly,
holy in its way.

It's washed in our bronze blood.

The Natural People

thrive
in that they journey in
the storm's surplus
& die

it's what they choose
the chaff
the moon

lodged in a frozen center
they lift a finger to touch
& snuff it

Proem

the end is the end
we hate it but for different reasons
a shadow moves over California's open edge
its valley full of people
but you compare the others to this one
filled to the brim with fog and people
I see their fires
trash slumbers
a blithe slumber, vibe of the beach
where everybody waits it out
strides into vacant flats
then fingerlike lies down
I look into its mouth
its bunch of bodies forming
it wants me to admit that I came here
and was drawn into its story
but no story draws me in
or one that no one understands
or the earth only

there is a shadow life
it can take you quite literally out of yourself
nowhere to go, no other home, no city
the water draws back from the shore's
undulant scoriae
pegged with shells of horseshoe crabs   *mini-society*

the mountain is up high, the shore down below
and the yet and the so and the or
the second more revanchist face   *forming*
it's impossible not to think of it
this other world is so close   *its circumference*
this wave that gathers
and answers my house   *built from a wrecked ship's timber*
this voice that whispers to itself
of a presence in the future   *a glory coming always*
always coming to obliterate
our history   *a chord of vicious beauty and duration*
in which anything was possible

    our work, rendering the nude

I supervise my thoughts for years
my old-time religion   *without edge or hinge*
though it may go nowhere
it may languish forever in the shadow of   *her prison tattoo, unmanageably erotic*
the grim brunette   *even bees like to balance there*
a muffler rusted through in weeds
the joint smoldering in the ashtray   *and guys devout as needles*
of my sister's Sentra, 1994
these are just teenage things
I watch myself become susceptible to the world
illegal on a farm all summer   *it's Greece they can live outdoors*
inspecting the bay in an open boat   *collecting mussels among the rocks*
sometimes like an eagle watching
lights through parlour windows

hollering halloa how are ye   *painting the sea, repeatedly*

through the glaciated valley

conjuring those that flared, eagle-like

and went down under   *flames looped over a log, or*

the wave's debris on fire

it can be done without the people there

if you have something of theirs   *steam from their horses' snouts*

all you need is their body, their face, their hair   *the steam of their necks*

a voice like a doctor's, anonymous but intimate

flowing through the valley's

open edge

byzantine subdivisions   *the city in potentia*

when it stops talking your house is gone   *merely timber, water, poetry*

permaculture torched, soil leached

your feet touch the fields they burn

smoke columns where trees were

shamanic   *open at both ends and deep*

the elderly Germans have a word for it

which is totally untranslatable

though I tell you

all throughout the valley people shout

Amen Hallelu

where you been

people push each other in the same direction

I go mostly where I'm led

people were with their friends when they were

swept into the water

headmaster, teachers all

were swept into the sea

it took forever

like they were hacking a path through the water

toward the deeper water

my neighbor says he became a monk

to bless my sister's soul

though I don't believe in any of that

so I say ehh I don't really believe in that

and I leave

my dog Geraldine follows me out

her jaws cradling the moon

how it rises huge and green

in the sky each night

over this chain of oval lakes

small muscles around her eyes and mouth

the survivors

the mutants that succeed us

what they do comes natural

they go back across the dark lake

they hack it

this valley is their house and

they can never leave this house

Geraldine sighs and lies down

the birds begin an hour before sunup

workers pull the tarps back
start up the saws
you know it's going to go on like this
not a paradise but what precedes it
the sound of the orchestra tuning
squat, ugly, unstoppable

James Capozzi is the author of *Country Album* (Parlor Press), which won the New Measure Poetry Prize. He's been the recipient of the New Letters Prize for Poetry, as well as fellowships and residencies from the James A. Michener Foundation, the Vermont Studio Center, the Woodstock Byrdcliffe Guild, Benaco Arte, and Joya: AiR. He lives in New Jersey, where he teaches at County College of Morris and edits the *Journal of New Jersey Poets*.

CPSIA information can be obtained
at www.ICGtesting.com
Printed in the USA
BVHW071106290719
554566BV00015B/1920/P